Creating Effective Language Lessons

Jack C. Richards
and David Bohlke

CAMBRIDGE UNIVERSITY PRESS
Cambridge, New York, São Paulo, Mexico City, Tokyo, Singapore,
Madrid, Cape Town, Dubai, Melbourne, New Delhi

Cambridge University Press
32 Avenue of the Americas, New York, NY 10013-2473, USA

www.cambridge.org

© Cambridge University Press 2011

This book is in copyright. Subject to statutory exception
and to the provisions of relevant collective licensing agreements,
no reproduction of any part may take place without
the written permission of Cambridge University Press.

First published 2011

Printed in the United States of America

ISBN 978-1-107-91202-1 Paperback

Book layout services: Page Designs International

Table of Contents

1 Examing an effective language lesson 1

2 Creating a positive learning environment 15

3 Developing learner-centered teaching 25

4 Planning and reviewing your lessons 35

Conclusions 43

References and further reading 44

1 | Examining an effective language lesson

Each time you enter your classroom, you set out to teach an effective lesson. You want to present a lesson that motivates your students, provides useful and relevant language practice, and helps the learners gain confidence in using English. But how can these goals be achieved? The nature of effective lessons and the way in which teachers create them is not always clear. Two teachers may teach the same lesson from a textbook or from a similar lesson plan, yet go about it very differently. Despite the fact that each teacher has his or her own individual teaching style, both lessons may be quite effective. And sometimes learners may enjoy a lesson a great deal even though the teacher's impression is that that the lesson failed to achieve its goals. On the other hand, a teacher may feel that he or she covered a lesson plan very effectively, yet the students appear not to have learned very much from it.

Task 1

What, in your opinion, are the essential characteristics of an effective lesson? List three or four below.

In this booklet, we will examine a number of essential characteristics of good teaching in an attempt to throw some light on what we consider to be an effective lesson. We will explore some of the thinking, skills, and practices that expert teachers employ in the classroom. We will also invite you to share your ideas and experience with others as we take a closer look at the nature of effective language teaching. To do this, we will begin by discussing what we see as eight principles of an effective language lesson.

1. Your lesson reflects high professional standards.

Language teaching, like other professions, is built around standards. Standards reflect the methodology that language teachers should know, the teaching skills they should possess, and the behavior they are expected to exhibit in their classrooms. Most schools would not hire someone who had a poor command of English, who had no professional training, and who dressed and behaved badly. These are not the standards expected of language teachers. Many schools and ministries of education have official documents that describe the standards that are expected of their teachers. For example, one country's Ministry of Education has described 18 standards for English teachers. The following examples are from the domain called *Planning and Management of Learning*:

- The English teacher uses a variety of instructional strategies and resources appropriately.
- The English teacher plans instruction according to the Ministry's educational goals, English curriculum, and assessment framework.
- The English teacher adapts instruction to take into account differences in students' learning styles, capabilities, and needs.
- The English teacher plans activities that will assist students in developing language skills and strategies.

Your professional standards will be reflected in many aspects of your teaching – for example, by the degree of knowledge and skill that is demonstrated in your teaching, by the extent to which your lessons reflect careful planning, and by the extent to which you control your emotions in the classroom. A teacher's interaction with his or her students must be respectful and appropriate at all times and should take into account each individual's age, gender, culture, and religion. Maintaining professional standards is crucial both inside and outside the classroom and is also reflected in your use of language and the way you dress.

Task 2

What professional standards are expected of language teachers at your school or institution? List some examples below.

2. Your lesson reflects sound principles of language teaching.

A good language lesson consists of much more than a series of activities and exercises that the teacher has strung together to occupy classroom time – and it involves much more than simply presenting the material in your textbook. Language teaching is not only a field of practical activity but also a discipline that draws on a considerable body of knowledge and practice. There are long traditions of theory, research, and practical experience to support contemporary approaches to language teaching. For this reason, teachers entering this educational specialization are required to acquire professional qualifications in order to assure that they are provided with a solid understanding of their subject. Such qualifications may range from entry-level training, such as a certificate course; more advanced courses at the diploma level; or courses such as the Teacher Knowledge Test. Individuals interested in pursuing this profession may also later wish to acquire a master's-level qualification, of which there are many available today. You may have been trained to teach according to a particular methodology – such as Communicative Language Teaching (CLT), Content and Language Integrated Learning (CLIL), Text-Based Teaching, or Task-Based Instruction (TBI); alternatively, you may have been introduced to a variety of teaching approaches and encouraged to use and adapt them to correspond to the kind of teaching situation you are in.

Regardless of the level of a teacher's qualifications, a good language lesson should reflect the specialized thinking and knowledge of an educated language-teaching professional. Every one of a teacher's lessons should reflect a solid understanding of the nature of language, of second-language learning and teaching, and of his or her learners – taking into account their needs as well as their learning styles and preferences.

Regardless of the type of training you have experienced, it is important for teachers to be familiar with current instructional methods and their underlying principles as well as with effective classroom techniques, materials, and assessment strategies appropriate to the type of course and the type of students you will be teaching. Clearly, your preparation will need to be customized according to the focus of the class – be it a reading course, a conversation course, a vocationally oriented course, a course for adults, or a course for young learners. Alternatively, you may be teaching in a program for English for Specific Purposes (ESP) or English for Academic Purposes (EAP).

Task 3

How would you describe the methodology that you use in your teaching? What principles is it based on? Describe it below.

3. Your lesson addresses meaningful learning outcomes.

Every lesson you present sets out to teach something, that is, to achieve one or more learning outcomes. The following are examples of outcomes for three different lessons:

- Students will learn how to write paragraphs containing a thesis statement and supporting ideas.
- Students will learn how to use concessive clauses.
- Students will learn the use of note-taking skills in academic listening.

Outcomes such as these refer to the skills or competencies that the students need to master. At the end of a lesson or of a unit, it should be possible to assess the students' improvements in the targeted skill(s).

Other learning outcomes address processes and learning experiences rather than specific competencies or observable outcomes. The following are some of the long-term goals commonly established for language teachers:

- To help students develop a positive attitude toward language learning
- To provide students with a successful experience in language learning
- To encourage students to work productively and cooperatively
- To give students control over their own learning

Therefore, as seen above, language-learning goals and outcomes may be both long term and short term. While long-term goals are usually determined for you by the syllabus or teaching materials that you have been assigned, teachers should also develop their own individual goals and outcomes for their lessons. These should be things you can identify, that you have thought about and planned for in some way. It has been shown that it can be valuable to share your goals with your students so that they come to realize that your teaching is planned and purposeful. To go about this, you might write your goals on the board at the beginning of each lesson to help students see the objectives that the lesson is planned to achieve.

A lesson's goals or intended outcomes will reflect the kind of lesson that you teach. The essential components of a speaking lesson will vary widely, for example, depending on the students' current level of proficiency and the stage they are at in their course. The initial stages of a beginning-level speaking course, for example, may focus on mastering greetings, introductions, and small talk in English, while the contents of an intermediate speaking course will usually include functions such as giving opinions and expressing agreement or disagreement, as well as taking part in discussions and interviews. The goals of a course may be both general and specific, as we see in the following examples of goals for a speaking course:

- The course practices speech features that the students will need outside of class.
- The students learn to use communication strategies.
- Students can discuss a wide range of topics in English.
- Students learn how to maintain communication in English through the use of questions and other turn-taking skills.
- Students expand their spoken vocabulary.
- Students are aware of problems in pronunciation and accuracy.

A useful way of stating lesson or course outcomes is in the form of the "can-do" statements found in the Common European Framework of Reference for Languages (CEFR). These describe what learners are able to do at different points along their learning path. For example, at Level A1 on the CEFR scale (a basic user), outcomes such as the following are described:

- I can use simple phrases and sentences to describe where I live and people I know.
- I can ask and answer simple questions in areas of immediate need or on very familiar topics.

With a set of can-do statements as a reference point, both the teacher and the learners can focus on using English for meaningful communication.

Creating Effective Language Lessons

Task 4

Describe some outcomes you hope for in one of the classes you regularly teach, such as a writing course or a speaking course.

- to keep convo going
- to initiate meaningful convo
- body language / face awareness

4. Your lesson provides opportunities for your learners to take part in extended practice with using language in a meaningful way.

Here are some important questions that you need to think about whenever you teach a lesson:

- What kind of language-learning opportunities did the lesson provide?
- How many opportunities were there for students to practice meaningful use of the language?
- Who had most of the opportunities for language use during the lesson – the teacher or the students?
- Did all of the students participate in the lesson, or did some students have more opportunities for participation and practice than others?

Teachers generally enjoy their time in the classroom, and teaching from one perspective is a kind of performance. However, it is important to remember that "performing" is not the key goal of teaching (Senior 2006). Facilitating student performance is a more important goal. One way of increasing the amount of student participation during a lesson is to vary the grouping arrangements that you use; in this way, you do not always dominate the lesson. The use of pair work and group work is one method that has been shown to ensure that students participate actively in a lesson. (See Chapter 2 in this booklet.) Another way to facilitate student performance is to make sure you call on all the students in the class when you ask questions – for example, by having a class list in front of you and checking off each student's name every time that you ask him or her a question.

Changing the class seating arrangement from time to time can also help to increase student participation; doing this will ensure that the students near the front of the class don't get more opportunities to participate than students who sit at the back. If you use group work on a regular basis, it is also useful to change the membership of the groups so that students have the chance to interact with a range of classmates and not only the ones they regularly talk to.

Another strategy that experienced teachers use is to give as many opportunities as possible for the learners to take responsibility for some of the regular class activities. For example, if you need to read out the correct answers to a homework assignment, consider asking one of the students to do it.

When thinking about the best way to go about teaching a particular lesson, carefully consider ways to ensure that your lesson plan includes as many opportunities for student practice as possible. (See Chapter 4.) At the end of the lesson, review the amount of student participation and practice that it provided.

Task 5

How do you ensure that your students have sufficient opportunities for individual practice of new learning items? Describe some strategies that you use.

5. Your lesson is effectively managed.

An important aspect of a successful lesson is the extent to which you are able to create a positive environment for learning. The term *classroom management* refers to ways in which you arrange both the physical and the social dimensions of the class in order to provide a supportive environment for teaching and learning (Wright 2005). No one can teach or learn effectively if the students are noisy and do not pay attention, use disruptive behavior, and do not treat their teacher or classmates with respect. Good classroom management is a prerequisite to an effective lesson. In some classes, a very supportive and positive atmosphere is immediately recognizable: Students are relaxed and focused, and work well together as a group or community. In other classes, it is evident that the students have no desire to be there and make little effort to support their teacher or classmates.

These dimensions of a lesson have to do with the ethos, or climate, of the class. Achieving a positive atmosphere depends on how the teacher and the students build up a sense of rapport and mutual trust. An important aspect of classroom management involves the procedures that a teacher can employ to organize student behavior, movement, and interaction in order to avoid disruptions to the flow of the lesson. When dealing with a new class, routines need to be quickly established. Experienced teachers have a repertoire of procedures at their fingertips that enable them to arrange student groups, to handle equipment and lesson procedures, and to respond to interruptions and disruptions appropriately. Teachers deal with management issues differently, depending on the kind of class they are teaching, their relationships with their students, and their own individual teaching style.

Task 6

Describe some typical classroom management challenges that you encounter in your teaching. How do you deal with them?

6. Your lesson is a coherent sequence of learning activities that link together to form a whole.

A language lesson consists of a sequence of activities that lead toward your lesson goals or objectives. The structure of a lesson is determined by how you deal with three essential stages of a lesson: openings, sequencing, and closings.

Openings.

This phase of the lesson serves primarily to focus the students' attention on the aims of the lesson, to make links to previous learning, to arouse interest in the lesson, to activate background knowledge, or to preview language or strategies students may need to understand in order to complete activities in the lesson. There are various ways in which a teacher can achieve a successful opening – for example:

- Ask questions to assess the learners' background knowledge or to develop ideas related to the topic.
- Use brainstorming and discussion activities.
- Show a DVD or video clip related to the lesson theme.
- Give a short test.
- Do or show something unusual to arouse students' interest in the lesson.

Sequencing.

A lesson is normally devoted to more than one type of activity, and teachers often have a "script" or preferred sequence that they follow when teaching a particular type of lesson, such as a speaking lesson, a reading lesson, a writing lesson, or a listening lesson. A common lesson sequence found in many traditional language classes consists of a sequence of activities referred to as P–P–P: *Presentation*, (new language items are introduced), *Practice* (students complete guided practice activities using the new language), and *Production* (students take part in freer, more open-ended activities using the new language). In communicative language teaching, lessons often begin with accuracy-based activities and move toward fluency-based activities. Reading lessons often follow a format consisting of *Pre-reading*, *While-reading*, and *Post-reading* activities. Listening lessons follow a similar format. Conversation lessons often begin with controlled practice activities, such as dialog practice, and move toward open-ended activities, such as role plays. Lessons based on a task-based approach often follow a sequence consisting of *Pre-task activities, The task cycle, The language focus*, and a *Follow-up task*.

In addition to the lesson sequence suggested by the teaching approach you are using or by the particular language skill you are teaching, other more general considerations will also influence the stages into which you think a lesson should be divided, drawing on principles such as "easier before more difficult activities," "receptive before productive skills," or "accuracy activities before fluency activities." At the same time, when planning a lesson, you will need to consider how you will handle the transitions between the different sequences of the lesson.

Experienced teachers are very skilled at handling the transitions between the different parts of a lesson. They tend to mark the onset of transitions clearly – for example, by stating when one activity should end and when the next will begin; they also make use of a variety of procedures to avoid losing class time as they move from one activity to another – for example, by implementing clear procedures for forming groups and for carrying out group work.

Less experienced teachers, on the other hand, tend to blend activities together, not paying sufficient attention to the links between events and taking too long to complete the movement between segments of a lesson. It is important to keep in mind that effective lesson links or transitions help maintain students' attention during transition times and establish a link between one activity and the next. Planning for transitions involves thinking about how the momentum of the lesson will be maintained during a transition – for example, while moving from a whole-class activity to a group-work activity; another issue that teachers need to consider is what students should do between transitions – for example, if some students complete an activity before the others.

Closings.

The closing phase of a lesson is also an important part of a lesson sequence. Ideally, it should leave the students feeling that they have successfully achieved a goal they set for themselves or that had been established for the lesson, and that the lesson was worthwhile and meaningful. Sometimes you and your students may have a different understanding of what you were trying to achieve in a lesson. At the end of a lesson, it is usually valuable to summarize what the lesson has tried to achieve, to reinforce the points of the lesson, to suggest follow-up work as appropriate, and to prepare students for what will follow. It is always important to praise the students for their effort and performance. During the closing stage, students may raise issues or problems that they would like to discuss or resolve; at this time, you may also encourage them to ask you for suggestions concerning how they can improve.

It is often useful to make students aware of the sequence or structure you have planned for a lesson. One way to achieve this is to write a brief lesson outline on the board before the lesson begins (preferably before the students come to class), listing the activities that the students will take part in and the purpose of each activity. This lets the students know what they will be expected to do during the lesson. It also gives students a sense that they are taking part in a lesson that has been well planned and organized. Another benefit of making sure everyone knows exactly how the lesson will play out is that late-coming students can be oriented to which part of the lesson has already been taught.

Task 7

Describe some effective ways of opening and closing a lesson.

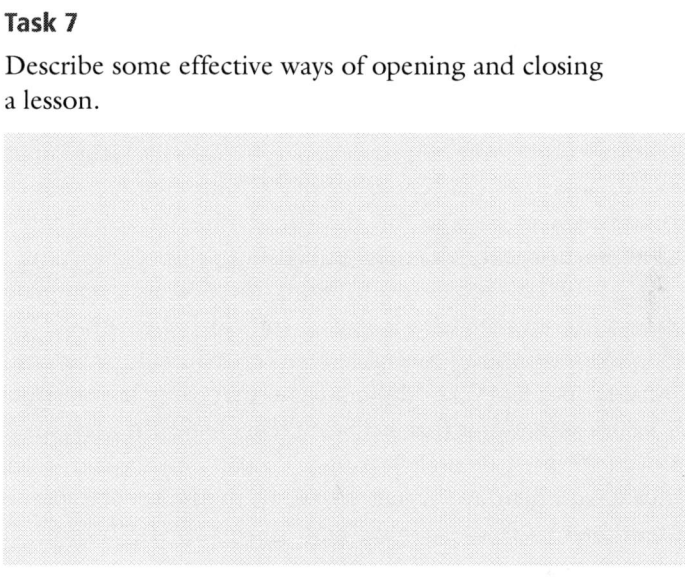

7. Your lesson creates a motivation to learn and provides opportunities for success.

Some learners look forward to their language class. Others dread going to class because they anticipate being engaged in activities that are not enjoyable, that appear to have little purpose, or that leave them feeling frustrated and/or embarrassed. As a teacher, you play a crucial role in developing a classroom atmosphere that encourages and motivates students in their learning. Perhaps you can recall the most inspiring language teachers you had as a student, and what made these teachers different and special. Among the qualities of exceptional language teachers are their enthusiasm for teaching, the high expectations they set for their learners, and the relationships they have with their students (Dornyei 2001).

Enthusiasm can be communicated in many different ways. If your students sense that you are positive and enthusiastic about the textbook or other materials that you are using, for example, they are likely to share your enthusiasm. Expectations for student success can be achieved through praising students' performance, by giving help to weaker students when needed, and by demonstrating the belief that one teacher expressed as "Every student in my class is a winner!" Establishing and exhibiting a warm, caring attitude toward students also contributes to building a positive class atmosphere. It has been shown that students who are treated as people and not just as numbers are generally more successful learners than those in classes where learners feel anonymous. It is important for teachers to learn their students' names and show interest in them as individuals.

Teachers also have an important role in building good relationships among their students. This involves working toward a sense of cooperation – rather than competition – among students, using group census-building activities and avoiding activities that could lead to strong disagreement or tension. It is also a good idea to engage the class in identifying acceptable norms of behavior and interaction – for example, establishing rules concerning punctuality and the use of cell phones, or determining the best way one group or pair member can support another who is having difficulty with a task. In addition, you can build in opportunities for success rather than failure by ensuring that tasks are at an appropriate level of difficulty and that every lesson contains some "take-away" value, something that helps students leave the class knowing that they have moved forward in their learning. "Take-away" value is achieved by reviewing your lesson plan in advance to assure that you have given sufficient time and attention to the most important aspects of the lesson. This could result in students' growing sense of confidence in writing a paragraph, in using some appropriate expressions to communicate with friends and neighbors, in understanding a list of ten or more useful vocabulary items, and so on.

It is also important to work toward maintaining the motivational level of the class. You can do this by asking yourself questions like the following:

- Do I vary the way I teach my lessons?
- Do I include activities that are there primarily to maintain motivation (for example, songs and language games)?
- Can I find ways of making my tasks more interesting (for example, by presenting a reading text as a jigsaw reading)?
- Can I increase the personal value of my lesson to my learners (for example, by adapting an activity so that it centers on the students' lives rather than on characters in the textbook)?
- Can I build in more opportunities for success in my lessons (for example, by choosing activities that challenge but do not frustrate learners)?

Task 8

Describe some ways in which you seek to develop a positive motivation toward language learning during your lessons.

8. The lesson reflects your personal philosophy of teaching.

While your teacher-preparation courses have introduced you to different teaching methods and approaches, you need to learn how to teach in *your* way, based on the kind of person you are and how you see your role in the classroom (Bailey and Nunan 1996). This does not mean that you can abandon everything you have learned during your training. Rather, it means that as you gain experience, you need to interpret and understand what it means to be a language teacher and what values, beliefs, theories, and assumptions you will use to guide you in your teaching. Some of these beliefs will be confirmations and elaborations of theories and principles you studied in your training courses or that you have learned from workshops or magazine articles. Now you will have a chance to more fully understand the ways in which language learning develops in learners, the kinds of feedback that facilitates language learning, and directions to take in order to manage learning activities so that your students can benefit from working together on group tasks and projects.

You will also be developing your own personal theories and principles that you want to apply in your teaching. One common challenge that language teachers face is figuring out ways to motivate reluctant learners. Your own experience may cause you to arrive at some important principles related to this common problem. These might include:

- Make learning fun.
- Make learning relaxing.
- Make learning personal.

As you plan and deliver your lessons, you will undoubtedly encounter opportunities to build principles like these into your teaching. And these, along with your training, will determine the type of teacher you turn out to be.

Task 9

What are some of the principles that account for the way you teach? List them.

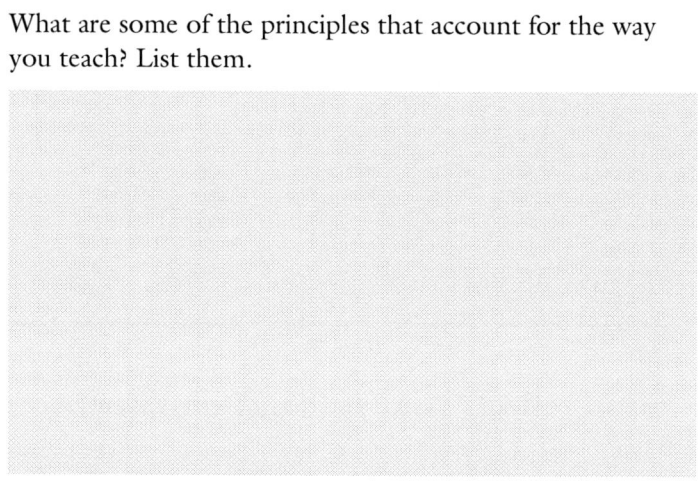

2 | Creating a positive learning environment

In this chapter, we will examine ways in which you can create a positive attitude toward learning in your classroom, and illustrate some of the strategies that effective teachers use to do this.

1. Create a positive classroom climate.

Classroom climate refers to the "affective" side of the classroom, such as the feelings the students have toward the lesson, toward the teacher, and toward their classmates, as well as the learning atmosphere of the classroom. As a teacher, you will need to find ways of helping your students develop a positive view of their class so that they have positive expectations for you and your lessons. Senior (2006) suggests the following ways in which teachers can create an effective classroom climate:

- Respect and care about your students as human beings.
- Establish a businesslike yet nonthreatening atmosphere.
- Communicate appropriate messages about the school subject matter.
- Give your students some sense of control with regard to classroom activities.
- Create a sense of community among your students.

Senior suggests other ways in which teachers can create a positive classroom climate – for example, by using humor to create an informal class atmosphere, by building rapport with the students through discussing common interests and concerns, and by showing that they are friendly and approachable and are there to help their students.

Additional factors that Senior discusses include creating a safe learning environment for students where they are not afraid to take risks or make mistakes, establishing professional credibility and a sense of purpose in lessons, and establishing appropriate norms of classroom behavior. The content of a lesson can also have an influence on classroom climate. If the lesson is too difficult, students may become bored and distracted. If the lesson is too easy, on the other hand, students may feel insufficiently challenged. In both situations, the results can be an unmotivated class.

Task 1

Describe some ways in which you try to create a positive climate in your classroom.

2. Arrange your class to promote effective learning.

While lesson plans represent a map of the territory you want to cover in a lesson and the route you want to take to get there, a successful lesson also depends on the kinds of interaction you provide for during the lesson. This will include opportunities for interactions between you and the class as well as interactions among the students themselves. There are four possible ways to arrange a class, with each offering different learning potentials: whole-class teaching, individual work, group work, and pair work.

Whole-class teaching.

This mode of teaching involves teaching all the students together; the extent to which you arrange your lesson for whole-class teaching will depend on the type of lesson you are teaching and on the particular stage of the lesson. A lesson may begin with a whole-class activity and then move to pair, group, or individual work. Whole-class, teacher-fronted teaching can serve to focus students' attention quickly on a learning task. When carefully carried out, it can lead to the quick and effective achievement of lesson objectives, since time management is maximally under the teacher's control. When planning your teaching, however, you will need to consider when whole-class teaching is appropriate and when you will make the transition to other types of learning in order to promote student-to-student interaction and allow students to work on tasks at their own pace.

Individual work.

There will also be points in a lesson where students will best work individually, such as when they are reading or listening to a text, or completing written exercises in a textbook or workbook. Individual work allows students to work at their own pace and to work on activities suited to their proficiency level or interests; having learners work on their own also allows you to provide them with individual support and/or assistance. In planning individual work, you will need to consider how well students understand what is expected of them and whether the task provides adequate challenge, support, and motivation to sustain their interest.

Pair work.

Pair work provides opportunities for sustained interaction and has long been recommended as a key means of promoting both accuracy and fluency in language use. Grouping students in pairs can take into consideration ability level, language and cultural background, and other factors that will facilitate a positive approach to learning. Students who are not familiar with this learning arrangement may need careful orientation and preparation for pair-work activities.

Group work.

Group-based learning is widely used in all forms of teaching and significantly changes the interactional dynamics of the classroom. In language classes, it increases students' talking time, helps promote self-esteem, and can increase student motivation by providing a risk-free environment for language practice. However, setting up group activities poses a number of challenges – for example:

> *Time*: The logistics of putting students into groups can be time-consuming.
>
> *Cliques*: Students often seat themselves in cliques by age, language group, friendship, and so on.
>
> *Limited language proficiency*: Low-level students may have difficulty following instructions or be intimidated working in a group with stronger students, causing them to remain silent.
>
> *Control*: Some teachers may feel that they are no longer in control of the class.

Successful implementation of group work involves the following considerations:

> *Group size*: Groups of four are easiest for ease of classroom management, especially for teacher-learners.

Group formation: You should select group members initially to achieve more of a heterogeneous mix that promotes peer tutoring and keeps the members focused on the task at hand.

Mixed proficiency levels: One way is to mix the groups with learners of different proficiency levels, as they can help one another with different tasks. Higher-proficiency students can be given more challenging tasks, such as acting as the group reporter or taking notes about the group's discussion.

Noise levels: One student in each group can be appointed as a monitor to keep the noise at acceptable levels.

Nonparticipants: Students who are unfamiliar with group work may not value group-based learning work. In this case, gentle persuasion may be needed.

Unequal completion times: Have a backup plan to limit the amount of disruption from groups who finish early – for example, an additional task for them to complete.

Monitoring group performance: The following guidelines are important:

- Pause regularly to visually survey the class as a whole, each group, and individual students.
- Keep visits to each group short so you can continuously observe everyone in class.
- Give students feedback to note when they are on track as well as off track.
- When students seem to be going in the wrong direction, look and listen to see what they are doing before jumping in.
- When you do intervene, comments should be intended to guide students back to the point at which they could do the work themselves.

When using a particular grouping arrangement, such as pair work or group work, it is important to make the purpose of the grouping arrangement clear to the students. Having students work in pairs or groups does not serve any useful purpose if the teacher continues to teach to the whole class despite the fact that students are in pairs or groups.

Task 2

Describe the strategies that you use in your classes to overcome any difficulties that come about as a result of group work.

3. Find ways of managing your use of class time.

Your classes may last from 40 to 50 minutes, but not all of that time is available for teaching and learning. You will often have procedural issues to attend to: returning assignments, discussing an activity you have prepared and describing how it is to be carried out, and so on. Some lessons have a good sense of pace and movement and maintain their momentum – an important part of retaining students' interest and motivation in the lesson. Other lessons progress too slowly. Richards and Lockhart (1994) cite a number of strategies that teachers can use to maintain the pace of a lesson:

- Avoid needless or overly lengthy explanations and instructions, and let your students get on with the job of learning.
- Use a variety of activities within a lesson, rather than spending the whole lesson on one activity.
- Avoid predictable and repetitive activities where possible.
- Select activities that are at the right level of difficulty.
- Set a goal and time for activities. Activities that have no obvious goal or conclusion or in which no time frame is set tend to have little momentum.
- Monitor your students' performance on activities so that they have sufficient time to complete them – but not too much time.

A useful way of thinking about the use of time in a lesson is through thinking of classroom time as consisting of the following four different categories:

Allocated time. This is the time allotted for teaching a class in the timetable, such as the typical 40- or 50-minute class period.

Instructional time. This is the time actually available for teaching after you have completed noninstructional activities: taking attendance, returning homework, and so on. In a 40-minute class period, perhaps 30 minutes of instructional time might be available.

Engaged time. This is that portion of time in which the students are actively involved in learning activities (also know as *time-on-task*). Perhaps it took some time for students to start the assigned activities since they spent some time chatting, organizing their desk or computer, assigning roles, and so on. Perhaps 25 minutes of the instructional time was actually engaged time.

Academic learning time. This is the amount of time during which students are actively engaged and participating in an activity and learning successfully from it. If an activity is too difficult or was not well set up, students may spend some time on ineffective learning routines and strategies before they finally find a successful way of completing the activity.

Task 3

List some ways in which you make maximum use of the learning time available during a lesson.

4. Maintain appropriate behavior in your classes.

In order to teach a successful lesson, there needs to be an atmosphere of respect and trust between teachers and students as well as a shared understanding of appropriate forms of classroom behavior. The class needs to develop a sense of community, of people working together cooperatively to achieve shared goals. This will not happen if students do not take the class seriously, if some students are allowed to disrupt the class with inappropriate talk or behavior, if students use their cell phones or send text messages during lessons, if students choose when it suits them to come to class or to start work on an assignment, and so on. A challenge for the teacher, especially one who is new to teaching, is to establish norms for appropriate classroom behavior so that the students develop a sense of responsible and cooperative behavior during lessons. Rather than adopting the role of discipline master, you should work with your students to establish an acceptable set of class rules that will allow for productive teaching and learning. This can be done in several ways – for example:

- Ask the students to discuss what they feel appropriate rules for classroom behavior should be.
- Propose different ways of dealing with classroom issues, and ask students to discuss them.

Of course the rules you establish should apply both to you and the students if you expect your learners to take the rules seriously. In one class, the teacher and students agreed that the door of the classroom would be locked once the lesson started. A few days later, the teacher arrived late for class and found that the students had locked the classroom door! Dornyei (2001) gives the following example of a set of class rules:

For the students
- Let's not be late for class.
- Always write your homework.
- Once a term you can "pass," that is, say that you have not prepared.
- In small-group work, only the L2 can be used.
- If you miss a class, make up for it and ask for the homework.

For the teacher
- The class should finish on time.
- Homework and tests should be marked within a week.
- Always give advance notice of a test.

For everybody
- Let's try and listen to each other.
- Let's help each other.
- Let's respect each other's ideas and values.
- It's OK to make mistakes; they are learning points.
- Let's not make fun of each other's weaknesses.
- We must avoid hurting each other, verbally or physically.

Task 4

List the rules that you establish in your classroom to avoid disruptive behavior during lessons.

---

5. Create a culturally sensitive classroom.

Second-language classrooms by their nature contain students with diverse cultural and educational backgrounds. Teaching students with different cultural backgrounds requires particular levels of sensitivity and awareness. Some of the characteristics of what can be called a culturally responsive classroom include the following:

> *Legitimizing students' cultures and experiences.* This can be achieved by inviting students to share information about their cultures and traditions and by showing a genuine interest in finding out more about them.

> *Including significant and comprehensive information about different cultures and their contributions in lessons.* This may involve adapting or supplementing topics from the textbook or curriculum to include information from the learners' cultures.
>
> *Using the cultural legacies, traits, and orientations of diverse students as filters through which they learn academic knowledge.* This may involve adapting teaching methods to accommodate the preferred learning styles of the students you teach.

In a culturally sensitive classroom, the teacher's goal is to shape the learning environment in such a way that it can accommodate a wide range of native languages, cultures, racial-ethnic backgrounds, religions, learning styles, and abilities. Dornyei (2001) offers a number of ways in which this can be accomplished, and suggestions like the following can help you to focus on the cultures represented in your classroom:

- Familiarize your learners with interesting/relevant aspects of the students' cultures.
- Develop your learners' cross-cultural awareness systematically by focusing on cross-cultural similarities (and not just differences) and by using analogies to make the strange familiar.
- Collect common stereotypes and prejudices about the second-language speakers, and discuss how valid these are.
- Share your own positive cross-cultural experiences in class.
- Collect quotations and statements by well-known public figures about the significance of language learning, and share these with your students.
- Ask your students to bring to class various cultural products (magazines, music, TV recordings, videos, and so on).
- Supplement your textbook with authentic materials.
- Encourage your learners to share interesting information about their cultures and to prepare a presentation.
- Arrange meetings with speakers from different cultures, and invite some interesting guests to your class.
- Organize class trips to different culturally distinct neighborhoods.

Task 5

Describe the ways in which you seek to build cultural awareness and sensitivity into your lessons.

3 Developing learner-centered teaching

An important skill in teaching is the ability to make your learners the focus of your teaching. This involves understanding your learners' needs and goals, communicating trust and respect for them, acknowledging that your students have different needs and learning styles, giving feedback on their learning in ways that help develop their confidence and self-esteem and minimize loss of face, and using strategies that help develop an atmosphere of collaboration and mutual support among learners (Dornyei 2001). In some lessons, the focus is more on teacher performance than on learner engagement, as is reflected in the following aspects of the lesson:

- The amount of talking you do during the lesson
- The extent to which input from learners directs the shape and direction of your lesson
- The extent to which your primary preoccupation during your lesson is with such things as classroom management, control, and order
- The way in which you present information and explain tasks
- The extent to which the lesson reflects your lesson plan

Some teachers, however, achieve a more learner-focused approach to teaching, as is reflected in features such as these:

- The degree of engagement learners have with your lesson
- The quantity of student participation and interaction that occurs
- The learning outcomes that the lesson produces
- The ability to present subject matter from a learner's perspective
- How well the lesson addresses learners' needs
- How you reshape the lesson based on learner feedback
- How you respond to learners' difficulties

Experienced teachers are often better able than novice teachers to create learner-centered teaching because they are familiar with typical student behavior. They use their knowledge of learners to make predictions about what might happen in the classroom, build their lessons around students' difficulties, and maintain active student involvement in lessons (Lynch 2001). Experienced teachers are able to recognize that language learning is not necessarily a direct consequence of good teaching but depends on understanding the different ways in which learners learn; on the role of individual learning styles, motivations, backgrounds, and purposes in learning; and on the fact that teaching needs to be adapted to their students' individual as well as their collective needs.

Learner-centered teaching is more effective than other modes of teaching for several reasons (Benson 2001) – for example:

- It is sensitive to individual needs and preferences.
- It encourages construction of knowledge and meaning.
- It draws on and integrates language learning with students' life experiences.
- It generates more student participation and target language output.
- It encourages authentic communication.
- It breaks down barriers between in-class and out-of-class learning.
- It opens up spaces for discussion of motivations, learning preferences, and styles.
- It encourages students to take more personal responsibility for their learning.
- It challenges the view that learning is equivalent to being taught.

We will now explore several ways in which learners can become the focus of your teaching.

1. Understand your learners' needs and goals.

Language classes consist of many different kinds of learners – some with similar needs and goals, and some with a great diversity of needs. The students in your class may be fairly homogeneous in nature, with students of a similar age and educational background, and with similar goals: for example, a class of students preparing for college or university. Conversely, you might find yourself teaching a very different kind of class, with students of different ages, interests, nationalities, cultural and educational backgrounds, and needs. You may have already developed a comprehensive profile of your students' needs. This may include the following kinds of information:

- The reasons your students are taking your course
- Your students' learning goals as well as their long-term goals
- Your students' attitudes toward learning English
- Your students' occupations
- Your students' cultural backgrounds

- Your students' current proficiency level(s)
- The ways in which your students use English outside the class
- Your students' main language difficulties

Where this sort of information is not available, you can use a variety of means to get an understanding of your learners' needs and goals, including conversations with your students, classroom activities in which students discuss issues related to needs and goals, questionnaires, and journal and other forms of writing.

Task 1

Describe your learners' main needs.

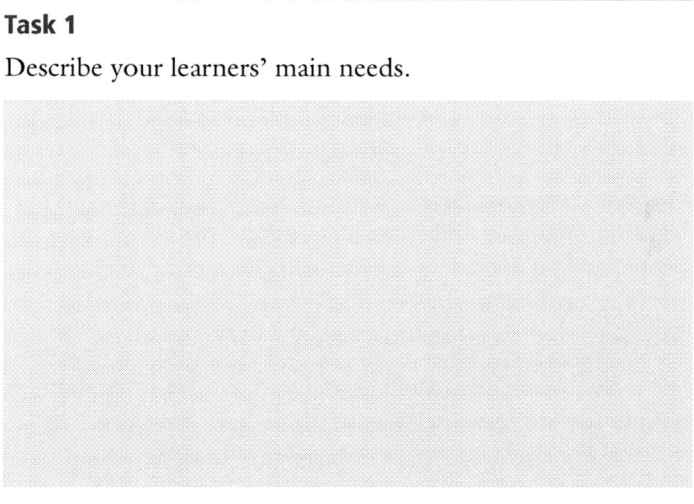

---

2. Understand your students' classroom participation styles.

Any language class will contain a mix of students with different dispositions toward learning. For example, the following six different types of students are sometimes found in a class, each of which favors a different style of classroom interaction and participation:

> *Task-oriented students.* These students are generally highly competent and successful in completing tasks. They enjoy learning, are active learners, aim for high levels of performance, are cooperative, and create few discipline problems.
>
> *Social students.* These students place a high value on personal interaction, and although competent in accomplishing tasks, tend to place a higher value on socializing. They enjoy working with others, may be talkative and outgoing, and do not hesitate to ask for assistance from the teacher or others when needed.

Dependent students. These students need constant support and guidance to complete tasks. They tend not to favor group work and often depend on the teacher or other students to tell them if their learning has been successful.

Phantom students. These students do not draw attention to themselves, although they generally work steadily on tasks. They rarely initiate conversation or ask for help. Because they do not disrupt the class or other students, the teacher may not know them well.

Isolated students. These students set themselves apart from others and withdraw from classroom interactions. They may avoid learning by turning away from activities such as pair or group work. They are reluctant to share their work with others.

Alienated students. These students react against teaching and learning, and may be hostile and aggressive. They create discipline problems and make it difficult for those around them to work. Their learning problems may be related to personal problems, and they therefore require close supervision.

It is likely that the classes you teach contain a majority of students who have a positive attitude toward learning. You will also have developed an awareness of the kinds of learners that make up the class; that understanding will be able to advise you on how to interact with students who pose difficulties.

Task 2

Do any of the students you teach pose particular difficulties? If so, describe how you deal with them.

3. Understand your students' cognitive styles.

Your classes may contain students who approach language learning in different ways and whose educational background and language-learning experience have established a particular set of beliefs and preferences about how best to learn a language. This may be reflected in different ways – for example:

- Do they prefer a particular kind of classroom activity?
- Do they prefer a particular style of teaching?
- Do they prefer a particular classroom arrangement?
- Do they prefer to study particular aspects of language?
- Do they prefer a particular mode of learning?

These are referred to as differences in cognitive style (also known as learning style). So while some students enjoy games and role plays, others may feel that such activities do not have a real teaching goal. Some students may want the teacher to correct any mistakes in their pronunciation, while others may feel that pronunciation is less important than fluency. Some students may feel more comfortable when the teacher is engaging in whole-class teaching, while others may prefer group-based learning. There are also students who prefer learning from technology and media-based resources to learning from books and other print-based materials. Therefore, as a teacher, you should recognize that while you have your convictions about the best teaching principles, techniques, and learning approaches, so do your students.

The following cognitive styles have often been referred to in discussing learning-style preferences, and you may begin to recognize these in some of your learners (Richards and Lockhart 1994). They may also lead to different styles of classroom participation (see above):

Visual learners. These learners respond to new information in a visual fashion and prefer visual, pictorial, and graphic representations of experience. They benefit most from reading and learn well by seeing words in books and workbooks, and on the board. They can often learn on their own with a book, and they take notes during lectures to remember the new information.

Auditory learners. These learners learn best from oral explanation and from hearing words spoken. They benefit from listening to recordingsand from teaching other students, and by conversing with their classmates and teachers.

Kinesthetic learners. Learners of this type learn best when they are physically involved in the experience. They remember new information when they actively participate in activities, such as field trips or role plays.

Tactile learners. These learners learn best when engaged in hands-on activities. They like to manipulate materials and enjoy building, fixing, or making things as well as putting things together.

Group learners. These learners prefer group interaction and classwork with other students, and learn best when working with others. Group interaction helps them better learn and understand new material.

Individual learners. Learners of this type prefer to work on their own. They are capable of learning new information by themselves and remember the material better if they learned it alone.

Activities in which students write about or discuss their successful and less successful language-learning experiences can help you learn about your students' preferred cognitive styles and their choices for the kinds of teaching they expect or prefer. At times, they may have a very different understanding from yours. You can avoid misunderstanding by sharing with your students your reasons for choosing the kinds of activities you assign and the particular teaching approach that you use, rather than imposing them on your students without explanation.

Task 3

Do you think your students favor any particular cognitive styles? If so, describe how you respond to these in your teaching.

---

4. Create a community of learners.

Although learner-centered teaching involves understanding your learners as individuals and finding ways of addressing their individual needs and differences, a language class can also be thought of as a community of learners, that is, a group of people with shared goals, needs, and concerns. A student in a British classroom captured this sense of community when she said: "When I arrived to start English classes, it was like being in a big family. They help each other and try to understand." Thinking of a class as a community means seeing it as a place where the individual members of the class cooperate and collaborate to achieve their common goals. This leads to more productive learning. Senior (2006) comments: "The unique character of each language class is based on shared understandings about how individuals (including the teacher) typically behave, react, and interact with one another within the confines of the communicative classroom."

You can build a sense of community in your classroom in different ways (Dornyei 2001; Senior 2006). These include:

- Learn and use your students' names.
- Recognize your students' different cognitive styles.
- Help your students find learning partners and groups that they are comfortable with.
- Encourage interaction within the class.
- Encourage a sense of friendship among your students.
- Use small-group tasks regularly.
- Use activities that require cooperation and collaboration.
- Encourage your students to share interesting experiences and stories.
- Be sure to treat your students fairly.
- Seek consensus on ways of dealing with classroom-management problems.

Task 4

What are some ways in which you try to build a sense of collaboration and community in your classes? Describe them below.

Creating Effective Language Lessons **31**

5. Personalize your teaching.

When talking about personalizing teaching, we mean trying to center your teaching wherever possible on your students and their lives, concerns, goals, and interests. This can be achieved by linking the content of your lessons to your students' lives and by involving your students in developing or choosing that content. For example, in teaching narratives, while the textbook you are using will provide examples of what narratives are and will describe their linguistic and textual features, students sharing personal stories among themselves can be a powerful way of promoting genuine communication. In sharing accounts of their childhoods and discussing significant events or experiences in their lives, students will be prompted to practice and develop their communicative resources by asking questions, asking for clarification, responding with their experiences, and so on. However, it is also important to recognize that cultures have different perceptions of information that is considered suitable for public disclosure and that which is considered private. Age, income, marital status, and family might be considered suitable for public discussion in some cultures but not in others; therefore, particularly with adult learners, you need to be careful not to raise issues that might cause discomfort or embarrassment for some students.

Students can also be involved in generating lesson content. For example, they can work in groups to choose suitable topics for essay writing. Instead of using examples from the textbook to present a lesson on idioms, for instance, students can compile lists of idioms they have encountered out of class and bring their lists to class. They can also be encouraged to bring in books they would like to read for extensive reading exercises rather than having the teacher decide on these for them. For listening activities, the students can be encouraged to move away from the audio programs provided with books, and instead to listen to their favorite songs or watch TV shows and/or movies. You may even be able to assign specific TV shows for students to watch and then discuss these later in class.

Another way of personalizing your teaching is to try to make links with the real-life situations where your students use English. Will they have a chance to use English in job interviews, in sending e-mail messages, in shopping, in talking to their neighbors, at the medical clinic, and so on? Try to find out in what settings and for what purposes your students need English. Bring these situations into the classroom through role plays or through realia (catalogs, brochures, advertisements, and so on), and use the materials as the basis for activities that reflect the students' language use in the real world.

Task 5

Describe some ways in which you can connect your teaching to your students' personal lives.

6. Build learner-centered outcomes into your lessons.

In Chapter 1, we discussed the importance of planning your lessons around learning outcomes. In your teacher-training course(s), you probably studied ways of describing learning outcomes – by using statements of objectives or competencies as planning devices in teaching, for example. A reading lesson may address outcomes such as the following:

- Students will learn how to recognize and interpret formal cohesive devices for linking different parts of a text.
- Students will recognize the function of discourse markers in texts.

While describing outcomes like this can be a useful way of organizing the content of a lesson, lessons can also be thought of in terms of what the learners take away from a lesson and the outcomes they perceived for themselves. Dornyei (2001) suggests a number of ways in which the learning outcomes that you set can acknowledge learners' concerns:

- Include tasks that involve the public display or performance of the outcome. Activities such as role plays or presenting a poster that students have designed allow students to publicly display what they have learned.
- Make the results tangible. Visual or written summaries of what has been learned – for example, in the form of a wall chart or a mention in a class newsletter – can remind your students of what they have learned.

Creating Effective Language Lessons 33

- Celebrate your students' success: Find different ways of praising and rewarding students for successes in learning.

Task 6

Describe the strategies that you can use to ensure that your lessons contain learner-centered outcomes.

4 Planning and reviewing your lessons

Planning a lesson before teaching it is generally considered essential in order to teach an effective lesson, although the nature of the planning and the kinds of information included in lesson plans can vary greatly. Experienced teachers generally make use of less detailed lesson plans than novice teachers and often teach from a mental plan rather than a detailed written lesson plan (Richards 1998). Also, lesson plans often differ from the lessons that teachers using them actually teach, since there are sometimes good reasons for departing from a plan, depending on the way a lesson proceeds and develops. Reviewing your lessons on a regular basis is a very useful activity as it enables you to better understand what worked well and what didn't work so well, and why. In this chapter, we will consider procedures for both planning and reviewing lessons.

> **Task 1**
>
> Do you prepare a lesson plan for most of the lessons you teach? If so, describe the information the plan typically includes.
>
>

1. The textbook as a lesson plan

Schools make different uses of commercial textbooks in language teaching. In some settings, the textbooks *are* the curriculum and the lessons that teachers teach closely follow the content of the textbook. Particularly in situations where teachers are not native speakers of English, textbooks often provide the major source of input to language lessons. For teachers who have had limited training, the textbook and the accompanying teacher's manual are their primary teaching resources. In these situations, the textbook provides both teachers and students with a map that lays out the general content of lessons and a sense of structure that gives coherence to individual lessons as well as to an entire course. This can give learners a sense of autonomy, which dependence on daily or weekly teacher-prepared lesson handouts does not provide.

Experienced teachers, however, make much less use of textbooks, particularly if they are trained language teachers and fluent users of English, and instead rely more on teacher-made or authentic materials (Senior 2006). These materials may have the advantage of more closely addressing students' needs and interests, allowing the teacher to teach in a more creative and flexible manner rather than following the sequence of exercises found in a textbook. If these teachers do use a textbook, they tend to use it selectively, adapting it to meet their needs. These adaptations may involve the following:

Modifying content. Content may need to be changed because it does not suit the target learners, perhaps because of factors related to the learners' age, gender, occupation, religion, or cultural background.

Deleting or adding content. The book may contain too much or too little for the program. Whole units may have to be dropped, or perhaps sections of the book omitted. For example, the English course may focus primarily on listening and speaking skills, and hence, writing activities in the book will be omitted.

Reorganizing content. The teacher may decide to reorganize the syllabus of the book and arrange the units in what he or she considers a more suitable order. Alternatively, within a unit, the teacher may decide not to follow the sequence of activities in the unit but to reorder them for a particular reason.

Addressing omissions. The textbook may omit items that the teacher feels are important. For example, the teacher may add vocabulary or grammar activities to a unit.

Modifying tasks. Exercises and activities may need to be changed to give them an additional focus. For example, a listening activity may focus only on listening for information. It can be adapted so that students listen a second time for a different purpose. Or an activity may be extended to provide opportunities for more personalized practice.

Extending tasks. Exercises may contain insufficient practice, and additional practice tasks may be needed.

Task 2

In what ways do you adapt your textbook to make it suitable for your students' needs? Describe them below.

2. The nature of a lesson plan

Lesson planning serves a variety of purposes. One important purpose is to help you develop your abilities to select, structure, and organize lesson content into effective support for learning. In addition to the conceptual and cognitive processes activated through lesson planning, however, it also serves a number of other functions – for example:

- It provides a framework or "road map" for your lesson.
- It helps you think through and rehearse the teaching process.
- It provides a sense of security.
- It determines the sequence and timing of activities.
- It helps you realize your principles and beliefs.
- It provides you with a record of what has been taught.

Even if you are teaching from a textbook (which contains lessons that have already been planned), further planning is usually necessary to adapt the textbook to the teaching context and to supplement it based on the learners' backgrounds, interests, learning styles, and abilities, as we saw above. For example, you will want to consider the specific instructional objectives for the lesson and choose tasks and activities that address the language skills that the lesson addresses. You will need to think about the resources you will use in the lesson as well as how much time you will spend on different activities. Your plan may also include ideas on how you will monitor your students' understanding and learning.

Task 3

Describe the types of information that you find useful to include in a lesson plan.

3. Developing the plan

There are no simple formulas for lesson plans, because what constitutes an effective lesson will depend on many factors, including the content of the lesson, the teacher's teaching style, the students' learning preferences, the class size, and the learners' proficiency level. A lesson plan will reflect your assumptions about the nature of teaching and learning, your understanding of the content of the lesson (for example, what you have learned from your coursework about paragraph organization, the present perfect tense, or reading for main ideas), your role in the lesson and that of your learners, and the methodology you plan to implement (for example, cooperative learning, process writing, or a communicative approach).

Generally, however, a lesson plan will reflect decisions that you have made about the following aspects of a lesson:

- *Goals*: What the general goals of your lesson are
- *Activities*: What kinds of things your students will do during the lesson, such as dialog work, free writing, or brainstorming
- *Sequencing*: The order in which activities will be used, including opening and closing activities
- *Timing*: How much time you will spend on different activities
- *Grouping*: When your class will be taught as a whole and when your students will work in pairs or groups
- *Resources*: What materials you will use, such as the textbook, worksheets, or DVDs

Richard-Amato (2009) suggests that language lessons can be generally divided into the following five different phases:

> *Opening.* Links are made to previous learning, or the lesson is previewed.
>
> *Simulation.* A lead into the main activity is provided to create interest in the lesson.
>
> *Instruction.* The main activity of the lesson is taught.
>
> *Closure.* The lesson may be reviewed and future learning previewed.
>
> *Follow-up.* Independent work or homework is assigned.

Task 4

What are some ways of providing an interesting opening to a lesson? Give some examples.

4. The role of the lesson plan in teaching

As we have seen, teaching is much more than enacting a lesson plan; during the process of teaching, many individual decisions have to be made that shape the nature and progress of the lesson, and not all of these decisions can be planned for in advance. These unplanned decisions are known as "interactive decisions." They include decisions relating to the following issues:

- *Task effectiveness*: Are tasks and activities working effectively?
- *Language focus*: Is there a sufficient language focus to an activity?

- *Language support*: Do students need more language support for an activity (for example, additional vocabulary or grammar)?
- *Grouping*: Should the grouping arrangement be changed?
- *Interest*: Are the students interested, or should something be done to maintain motivation?
- *Sequencing*: Should the planned sequence be changed in any way?
- *Transitions*: Is a better transition needed between activities?
- *Pacing*: Should the planned timing be modified?
- *Difficulty*: Is the lesson proving to be at the right difficulty level?
- *Student understanding*: Is clarification needed?
- *Student behavior*: Is intervention needed to control noise levels or disruptive behavior?

A lesson plan should be regarded as a blueprint for action. In teaching your lessons, you will still have to "play it by ear" and teach according to the changing circumstances of the actual situation. Your lesson plan will therefore have to be renegotiated according to what occurs during the lesson itself.

Bailey (Bailey and Nunan 1996) studied the departures that six experienced ESL teachers made from their lessons during teaching. She describes the reasons for these departures in terms of the principles they hold about good teaching. The teachers gave the following justifications for departing from their lesson plans:

1. *Serve the common good.* For example, an issue raised by an individual student was thought to be worth pursuing because it would benefit the whole class.
2. *Teach to the moment.* For example, the teacher drops the lesson plan and pursues an issue likely to be of particular interest to students at that moment.
3. *Accommodate students' learning styles.* For example, the teacher decides to incorporate some explicit grammar instruction since the learners have a preference for this mode of grammar learning.
4. *Promote students' involvement.* For example, the teacher drops a planned activity to give students more time to work on an activity that they have shown a high degree of interest in.
5. *Distribute the wealth.* For example, the teacher keeps one student from dominating the class time to enable the whole class to benefit from a learning opportunity.

Task 5

What are some of the unplanned things that sometimes occur during your lessons? Describe how you deal with them.

5. Reviewing the lesson

After teaching a lesson, it is important to take time to review how well the lesson went. This involves asking questions such as the following:

1. Did my students enjoy the lesson?
2. Were there sufficient activities to engage my students throughout the lesson?
3. Which aspects of my lesson were the most successful? Which were the least successful?
4. Did I manage to achieve what I set out to teach? Were my objectives met? What evidence do I have for this?
5. What difficulties did my lesson pose?
6. Will I teach my lesson in the same way next time?

In thinking about questions like these after a particularly successful (or unsuccessful) lesson, it is useful to write a brief report from time to time. This could be either an entry in a teaching journal, a list of key points that you want to think about further, or annotations to your lesson plan. Whatever method you choose, such lesson reports can serve to trigger a better understanding of what worked well and why, or to prompt you to rethink a teaching strategy if aspects of the lesson did not turn out as well as you expected. Since every lesson you teach has a life of its own, you will often find that even if a lesson worked perfectly on one occasion, teaching it in the same way the next time may not have the same results. Teaching always involves adjusting your lesson plans according to the way the lesson evolves. In other words, it requires you to build a lesson around your plan based on the students' reactions to the lesson, rather than enacting your lesson plan based on your prior intentions for the lesson.

Conclusions

In this booklet, we have examined a number of factors that contribute to the effectiveness of a language lesson. Creating effective language lessons depends upon a number of factors, each of which can play a role in shaping the nature of a lesson. As we have seen here, effective teachers seek to meet high professional standards. In order to achieve this, they draw on their understanding of principles of effective teaching, they set clear outcomes for their lessons and plan their lessons carefully, they make use of strategies to manage their classes so as to facilitate successful teaching and learning, and they seek to make their learners the focus of their lessons.

Since teaching is a very personal activity and the strategies that good teachers use to create effective lessons will depend on a number of factors – such as the type of students the teacher is teaching, the class size, the teacher's experience and training, and the teacher's individual teaching style – there are no fixed rules and procedures for achieving successful language lessons. The key issue is the teacher's active, ongoing involvement and reflection on the processes of teaching and learning, leading to a deeper understanding of the nature of effective teaching and how it can be achieved. We hope that the issues discussed in this booklet will help you reflect on your own teaching beliefs and practices as you engage in the process of planning and teaching effective language lessons.

References and further reading

(Part of this booklet is adapted from Jack C. Richards and Thomas Farrell: *Practice Teaching – a Reflective Approach*. New York: Cambridge University Press 2011.)

Bailey, K. M. and Nunan, D. (1996). *Voices from the language classroom.* New York: Cambridge University Press.

Benson, P. (2001). *Teaching and Researching Autonomy in language Learning.* London: Longman.

Dornyei, Zoltan. (2001) *Motivational Strategies in the Language Classroom.* Cambridge: Cambridge University Press.

Farrell, T. S. C. (Ed.). *Classroom Management.* Alexandria, VA: TESOL Publications. 2008.

Farrell, T. S. C. (2002). Lesson planning. In J. C. Richards and W. A. Renandya (Eds.), *Methodology in language teaching: An anthology of current practice* (pp. 30–39). New York: Cambridge University Press.

Hadfield, J. (1992). *Classroom Dynamics.* Oxford: Oxford University Press.

Lynch, T. (2001). Promoting EAP learner autonomy in a second language university context. In J. Flowerdew & M. Peacock (Eds.), *Research Perspectives on English for Academic Purposes* (pp. 390-403). Cambridge: Cambridge University Press.

Richard-Amato, P. (2009). *Making It Happen: From Interactive to Participatory Language Teaching: Evolving Theory and Practice* (4th Edition) New York: Pearson.

Richards, J.C. and Lockhart, Charles (1994). *Reflective Teaching in Second Language Classrooms.* New York: Cambridge University Press.

Richards, J. C. (1998). *Beyond training.* New York: Cambridge University Press.

Scharle, Á. and Szabó, A. (2000). *Learner Autonomy: A Guide to Developing Learner Responsibility.* Cambridge: Cambridge University Press.

Senior, R. (2006). *The experience of language teaching.* New York: Cambridge University Press.

Woodward, T. (2001). *Planning lessons and courses.* Cambridge: Cambridge University Press.

Wright, Tony. (2005) *Classroom Management in Language Education.* Basingstoke: Palgrave.

In *Creating Effective Language Lessons* authors Jack C. Richards and David Bohlke examine the essential characteristics of good teaching that lead to the creation of effective lessons. By exploring the core principles and practices that expert teachers employ in the classroom, Richards and Bohlke outline the key principles that language teachers need to be familiar with in order to create and plan effective lessons while fostering a positive attitude toward learning in a student-centered classroom.

Jack C. Richards is an internationally renowned specialist in English Language Teaching and an applied linguist and educator. He is the author of numerous professional books for English language teachers as well as many widely used textbooks for English language students. His titles include the best-selling *Interchange* series, *Four Corners*, *Passages*, *Connect*, and *Strategic Reading*.

David Bohlke has over 20 years of experience as a materials writer, editor, language consultant, teacher, and teacher trainer. He specializes in creating fun, flexible, and easy-to-use classroom materials and has conducted multiple teacher training workshops around the world. He is also co-author of *Four Corners*.

www.cambridge.org

ISBN: 9781107912021